D0794454

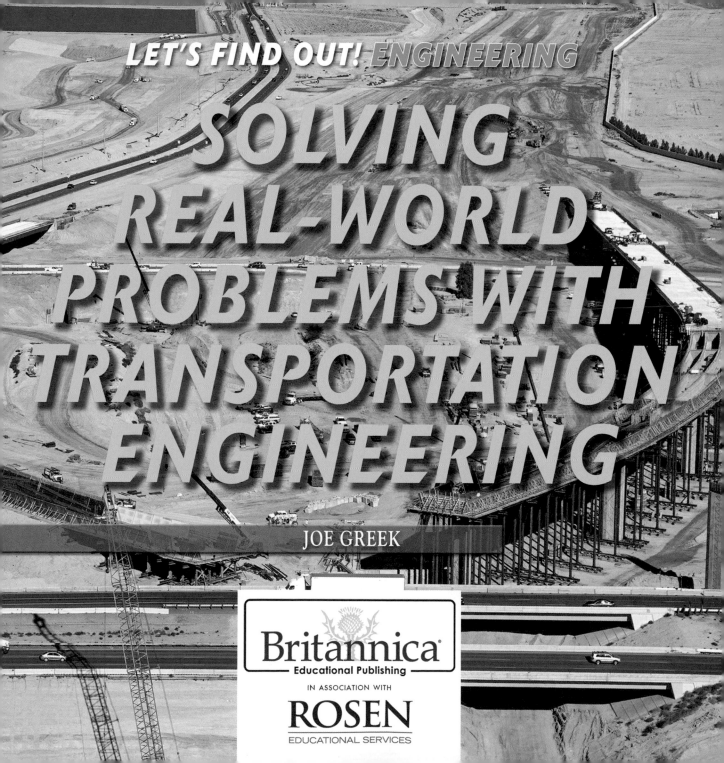

SOLVING REAL-WORLD PROBLEMS WITH TRANSPORTATION ENGINEERING

JOE GREEK

Britannica®
Educational Publishing

IN ASSOCIATION WITH

ROSEN
EDUCATIONAL SERVICES

Published in 2016 by Britannica Educational Publishing (a trademark of Encyclopædia Britannica, Inc.) in association with The Rosen Publishing Group, Inc.
29 East 21st Street, New York, NY 10010

Distributed exclusively by Rosen Publishing.
To see additional Britannica Educational Publishing titles, go to rosenpublishing.com.

First Edition

Britannica Educational Publishing
J.E. Luebering: Director, Core Reference Group
Mary Rose McCudden: Editor, Britannica Student Encyclopedia

Rosen Publishing
Philip Wolny: Editor
Nelson Sá: Art Director
Nicole Russo: Designer
Cindy Reiman: Photography Manager

Library of Congress Cataloging-in-Publication Data

Greek, Joe, author.
Solving real-world problems with transportation engineering/Joe Greek. — First edition.
      pages cm. — (Let's find out! Engineering)
Audience: Grade Level 1-4.
Includes bibliographical references and index.
ISBN 978-1-68048-262-1 (library bound) — ISBN 978-1-5081-0071-3 (pbk.) — ISBN 978-1-5081-0005-8 (6-pack)
1. Transportation engineering — Juvenile literature. I. Title.

TA1149.G74 2016
629.04 — dc23

2015033957

Manufactured in the United States of America

Photo credits: Cover, p. 1 © iStockphoto.com/Rinelle; cover and interior pages background Robert Adrian Hillman/Shutterstock.com; p. 4 James Steinberg/Science Source; p. 5 Print Collector/Hulton Archive/Getty Images; p. 6 Andrew Rakoczy/Science Source; p. 7 Robert and Jean Pollock/Science Source; p. 8 Earth Satellite Corporation/Science Source; p. 9 Dirk Wiersma/Science Source; p. 10 Spencer Sutton/Science Source/Getty Images; p. 11 Portland Press Herald/Getty Images; p. 12 Martin Shields/Science Source; pp. 13, 16 DEA/Archivio J. Lange/De Agostini/Getty Images; p. 14 DEA/C. Bevilacqua/De Agostini/Getty Images; p. 15 Theodore Clutter/Science Source; p. 17 Mint Images – Frans Lanting/Getty Images; p. 18 N. R. Rowan/Science Source; p. 19 David McNew/Getty Images; p. 20 Mark Garlick/Science Source; p. 21 Joe Tucciarone/Science Source; p. 22 George Bernard/Science Source; p. 23 Tommaso Boddi/WireImage/Getty Images; p. 24 © Aurora Photos/Alamy Stock Photo; p. 25 Phil Hill/Science Source; p. 26 Richard and Ellen Thane/Science Source; p. 27 Universal Images Group/Getty Images; p. 28 David R. Frazier/Science Source; p. 29 © Stephen Mulcahey/Alamy Stock Photo; interior pages (arrow) Mushakesa/Shutterstock.com

CONTENTS

WHAT IS TRANSPORTATION ENGINEERING?

Transportation is a general word for all the methods people use to move themselves and their goods from one place to another. Just as we have for thousands of years, people today rely on walking to travel short distances. For longer trips, people depend on automobiles, trucks, railroads, and airplanes.

Transportation engineers find ways to improve that travel. They design the layout of streets to help

Building a highway interchange is a very big project for engineers to plan and complete.

Projects like New York's AirTrain help meet the transportation needs of airline travelers.

us safely get from place to place. However, advances in transportation sometimes lead to problems. Cars and trucks cause traffic jams, accidents, and air pollution. To ease crowded roads, engineers design public transportation systems, such as subways. Without the work of transportation engineers, it would be difficult to get to school or to work.

THINK ABOUT IT

Transportation engineers are responsible for the roads we drive on. How long would it take you to get to the grocery store or school if there were no roads?

BEFORE THERE WERE ROADS

Cars, trucks, buses, motorcycles, and bicycles travel on strips of land called roads. Some roads are made of dirt or gravel. A firm, strong material called pavement covers most modern roads. Types of roads include city streets, country roads, and long-distance highways.

Before there were roads, people traveled by foot along trails. These paths were often used for hunting as well as to connect villages. Many trails were made at random by

A steamroller prepares roads for the 2016 Olympics in Rio de Janeiro, Brazil.

wandering animals. Sometimes people could wander away from the trails and become lost.

Today, engineers locate the best possible places to build roads. Roads are designed to reduce environmental harm and traffic. Also, modern roads are usually built to reduce the time it takes to travel between places.

COMPARE AND CONTRAST

In early times, goods were transported on trails and dirt roads by horse and wagon. In what ways do we transport goods by road today?

Engineers need to think about human needs and the environment when designing roads.

7

BUILDING ROADS

People in ancient Egypt and western Asia built the earliest roads more than 4,000 years ago. Later, the ancient Romans became famous as road builders. They built roads paved with stone across Europe. The roads they built were used for trade (that is, to sell goods) and to move military forces.

The ruins of Roman roads show how they have stood the test of time, partly due to Roman engineers' skills.

The Spanish built the first roads in North America along Native American trails. Early roads in colonial America were usually dirt, sometimes covered with rows of logs.

The construction of the American highway system was a massive feat of engineering.

As cars became popular in the early 1900s, people began building more roads paved with concrete and asphalt. In the 1950s the United States began building a system of large roads, called highways, across the country. Today, highways cross many countries, but some poor countries still have mostly unpaved roads.

THINK ABOUT IT

When designing roads, engineers and governments have to think about the safety of drivers and passengers. How do you think roads are made safer?

BUILDING BRIDGES

Roads help people travel from one point to another. Some obstacles, however, require the use of bridges. A bridge is a structure that people and vehicles use to cross over an open space. Bridges stretch across deep pits in the earth, bodies of water, and roads.

Early humans built bridges from logs, branches, or stones.

Many bridges help connect land masses separated by bodies of water.

> **Suspension bridges** are supported by large cables running between towers. Smaller cables connect the large cables to the road on each bridge, called a deck.

They also made suspension bridges with long, tough vines. The ancient Romans built many stone arch bridges that still exist today.

Modern bridge building began in the 1700s. People built bridges from iron and, later, steel. These metals were stronger and cheaper than stone. By 1850 some bridges were strong enough to support heavy trains. Concrete became a popular bridge material in the 1900s. Today, engineers continue to improve bridge-building techniques.

New York's Verrazano-Narrows Bridge is the United States' longest suspension bridge.

Obstacles: Things That Get in the Way

Natural obstacles—such as mountains, hills, or rivers—can block the path of a railway, highway, or pipeline. To fix this problem, transportation engineers dig tunnels through or under the obstacles.

The first known tunnel was dug in the ancient city of Babylon more than 4,000 years ago. It passed under the Euphrates River and connected a royal palace with a

The Channel Tunnel connects France and England. It runs under the English Channel.

temple. An early Greek tunnel was made in 687 BCE on the island of Samos. It was used to carry water. Tunnels that are used to transport water are called aqueducts.

Modern engineers use large drills, called tunnel-boring machines, to cut through soil and hard rock. Many cities, such as New York City, have underground train systems, called subways, which are used in mass transportation. Subways reduce the number of cars that are on city streets. Having fewer cars on roads also reduces pollution and traffic.

Mass transportation is the use of subways, buses, trains, and ferryboats to move many people from place to place.

13

CANALS AND WATER TRANSPORTATION

New York State's Erie Canal, which greatly improved trade, is depicted in this 1830 illustration.

Water is often used for transporting goods and people, sometimes over far distances. In turn, water often needs to be transported to people who need it. Engineers help solve the problem of water transportation by building canals.

Canals are waterways that are used for shipping, travel, and irrigation. Canals can be natural or human-made. They are an important mode of transportation.

Some canals make it possible for boats to travel inland from oceans and lakes. A canal may also serve as a shortcut between two bodies of water. Other canals carry drinking water to cities or irrigation water to farms.

COMPARE AND CONTRAST

We depend on water to survive. Compare and contrast the different ways that we use water.

The canals of Amsterdam, in the Netherlands, are one of that city's unique features.

Lock It Up

To make a canal, builders dig a long channel in the ground and fill it with water. The water usually comes from a connecting river, lake, or ocean. Builders often line the canal with stone, concrete, or steel to make it stronger. The lining also prevents the water from leaking out.

Locks are an important part of many canals, especially in areas where the land is not completely flat.

Locks are stretches of canals that are blocked off at each end by strong gates. These gates can be opened or closed to allow water to fill or to drain from the lock. Locks allow boats to travel between lower and higher areas of a canal.

A massive lock is transported during a 2015 expansion of the Panama Canal.

The world's oldest canal still being used today is the Grand Canal in China. It is also the world's longest canal, with a length of about 1,100 miles (1,770 kilometers). In Venice, Italy, people use canals as roadways. In the oldest parts of the city, people travel by boat instead of by car.

Venice, Italy, has perhaps the world's best-known system of canals.

ALL ABOARD!

A railroad, also called a railway, is a type of land transportation. Railroad cars travel along a path of two metal rails, or tracks. A train is a row of wheeled cars linked together. Rail car wheels have rims that keep them on the rails. Trains can be divided into two types: passenger and freight. Passenger trains carry people. Freight trains carry goods.

Before there were trains and locomotives, people used horses to pull carts along tracks. Europeans began using this early type of railroad in the 1500s to carry heavy loads to and from mines.

Thousands of workers spent several years building the first transcontinental railroad.

In the 1800s the first railroads were built. By 1869 railroads stretched across the whole of the United States, from the east coast to the west coast.

Engineers continue to build new kinds of trains. Maglev trains rely on magnetic forces. Magnetism holds the train above the rail and pushes it forward.

COMPARE AND CONTRAST

Trains and planes can carry many people across long distances. Compare and contrast the benefits of traveling by rail and by air.

THE USES OF PIPELINES

Pipelines carry liquids, gases, and slurries between places. The water we use for drinking and bathing travels through pipelines.

Pumps, valves, and other devices control the speed and amount of material moving through pipelines. Products such as fuel are held in storage tanks and other facilities. From there, they are

> Mixtures of small bits found in liquid—such as mud or cement—are called slurries.

New York's Water Tunnel No. 3 was a major engineering project.

sent through pipelines, often across long distances, to their destinations.

Pipelines are usually underground. They may carry materials that are dangerous to the environment, such as oil and sewage. Engineers therefore have to design pipelines to be secure and strong.

Despite the hard work of engineers in designing them, fuel pipelines can sometimes explode.

Many people oppose building and using pipelines. One example is the Keystone Pipeline, which carries oil from Canada to the United States. Its use is often debated because of potential environmental damage.

GOING UP, GOING DOWN

It would take a long time to walk up the 102 floors of the Empire State Building in New York City. Many people would not be able to climb all those stairs. Fortunately, there is a transportation invention called the elevator.

Elevators, or lifts, carry passengers and freight up and down. They are used in

The elevator is a common modern transportation method.

THINK ABOUT IT

Elevators help people move lower and higher. What other device that is often found in malls does something similar?

buildings, on ships, and even underground, in both private and public buildings.

The earliest version of an elevator was created by the ancient Greek scientist Archimedes. It was a basic hoist operated by ropes and pulleys. The first true elevator, however, was built in the 19th century. It used hydraulic power.

Modern elevators run on electricity and pull carts with steel cables. Mines use elevators to transport workers; some go more than a mile underground!

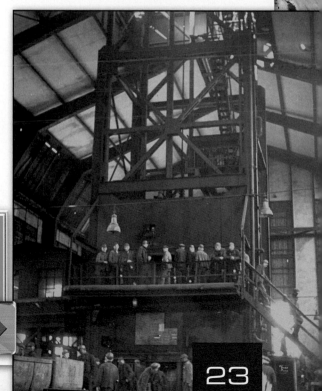

The coal industry was one of the first users of elevator technology.

TRANSPORTATION TERMINALS

The world depends on the mass transportation of goods and people. The food we buy at grocery stores often comes from different places around the world. Making sure that many goods and people arrive to their destinations requires distribution.

To make the distribution process better, engineers developed terminals. Terminals are central locations for mass

> The act of sending goods from one location to several destinations is called distribution.

New York City's Port Authority bus terminal is shown here.

A container ship unloads at a port in Hamburg, Germany. Trucks then haul away its freight.

transportation and distribution. For example, airports and bus stations are types of terminals.

For people, terminals are buildings where they board planes, buses, trains, and ships. Hartsfield-Jackson Atlanta International Airport is one of the busiest airports in the world. In 2014 more than 96 million passengers passed through the airport!

China's Port of Shanghai is the busiest shipping port in the world. Many of the products bought in US stores travel through this seaport before being shipped across the ocean to ports around the United States.

PEDESTRIAN AND BICYCLIST SAFETY

Each year thousands of pedestrians and bicyclists are killed by motor vehicles. To improve everyone's safety, engineers design sidewalks, crosswalks, bicycle lanes, and other safety measures.

Sidewalks are placed side-by-side with streets. These paths protect **pedestrians** from cars. Early sidewalks

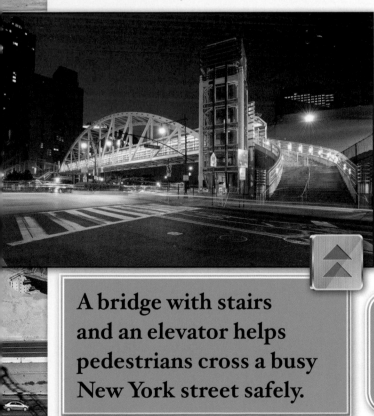

A bridge with stairs and an elevator helps pedestrians cross a busy New York street safely.

Pedestrians are people who walk from one place to another.

Even something as simple as a bike lane requires careful planning by traffic engineers.

separated pedestrians from wagons. The first sidewalks were built around 4,000 years ago in what is now Turkey. Modern ones are made from cement.

Pedestrians often use crosswalks when crossing busy city streets. There are even traffic signals that tell pedestrians when they can cross a road. Engineers also design pedestrian bridges spanning busy roads.

Many cities have traffic lanes just for bicyclists. With so many people choosing walking and biking over cars, pedestrian and bicyclist safety is more important than ever.

ENGINEERING IN ACTION

Millions of people everywhere use bridges. Bridges must be built strong to support a lot of weight safely.

Test your engineering skills by building a bridge using paper and paper clips. You will need 2 cups, plain paper, paper clips, and pennies.

Begin by placing two cups 8 inches (20 centimeters) apart. Lay a piece of paper across the two cups to form a simple bridge. Start

The High Bridge aqueduct, shown in 1925, transported water across the Harlem River.

placing pennies one at a time on the middle of the bridge. Keep track of how many pennies the bridge can hold before it falls.

Changing the shape of bridge material can make it stronger. Fold, twist, or roll the paper and see how many pennies it will support.

There are other ways to strengthen a bridge. Use paper clips to provide extra support to your paper.

Engineers cannot build numerous full-size bridges to test designs. They rely on models to make sure bridges will be strong.

How many pennies did your bridge hold?

A small model of a bridge obeys the same physical laws as a real one used by people.

GLOSSARY

aqueduct A system designed to carry water from one source to another.

cable A strong fiber or wire rope.

cement A powder that is made from a mixture of clay and limestone and is used to make concrete.

drill A device or machine with a rotating tip that forms holes in objects.

engineer A person who designs and creates ways to solve problems.

highway A main road that connects major towns or cities.

hoist A device that is used to lift objects up and down, such as a crane.

hydraulic power Energy that is created through the motion of liquids such as water.

inland Areas of a country that are located away from the coast or boundaries.

magnetism The property of attracting certain metals or producing a magnetic field.

mine A pit or tunnel from which minerals are taken.

pulley A wheel with a grooved rim used with a rope or chain to support movement and change the direction of a pulling force.

seaport A harbor along a coast within reach of ships.

subway An underground train system that is generally used to move people around a city.

valve A device that controls the flow of liquid, gas, or loose materials through a pipe.

FOR MORE INFORMATION

Books

Hurley, Michael. *The World's Most Amazing Bridges*. Chicago, IL: Raintree Publishing, 2011.

Leake, Diyan. *Canals* (Water, Water Everywhere). Portsmouth, NH: Heinemann, 2014.

Lyons, Shelly. *Transportation in My Neighborhood*. Mankato, MN: Capstone Press, 2013.

Philip, Ryan. *Subways* (All Aboard!). New York, NY: PowerKids Press, 2010.

Rustad, Martha. *Transportation in Many Cultures* (Life Around the World). Mankato, MN: Capstone Press, 2010.

Websites

Because of the changing number of Internet links, Rosen Publishing has developed an online list of websites related to the subject of this book. This site is updated regularly. Please use this link to access the list:

http://www.rosenlinks.com/LFO/Trans

INDEX